BLENDED FAMILIES

RECIPES FOR SUCCESS

Barbara J. Peters

Illustrated by Dave Garbot

Blended Families: Recipes for Success
Barbara J. Peters
Illustrated by Dave Garbot

Back cover statistics are from *Smart Stepfamilies*. (2016). Little Rock, AR: FamilyLife Blended. https://smartstepfamilies.com/
Make all inquiries at barbarajpeters.com

Cartoons by CartoonStock, used by permission, from artists Bradford Veley, Carroll Zan, and Martha Campbell; www.CartoonStock.com. Kitchen icons from Vecteezy: For Acceptance, Compassion, Flexibility, Communication, and Couple Intimacy, antohoho. For Finance and Write Me, Nadiinko. Banners from Vecteezy, Iuliia Voitkova. Interior photos by Shutterstock. Appetizers, AlexeiLogvinovich; Main Course, FREEPIK2; Sweet Course, Chakkraphan.

Publisher's Cataloging-In-Publication Data
(Prepared by The Donohue Group, Inc.)

Names: Peters, Barbara J. (Barbara Joyce), 1944- author. | Garbot, Dave, illustrator.

Title: Blended families : recipes for success / Barbara J. Peters ; illustrated by Dave Garbot.

Description: Alpharetta, Georgia : [Barbara J. Peters], [2022] | Includes bibliographical references.

Identifiers: ISBN 9780578336008 (paperback) | ISBN 9780578336022 (ebook)

Subjects: LCSH: Stepfamilies. | Interpersonal relations. | Communication in families. | Intimacy (Psychology)

Classification: LCC HQ759.92 .H35 2022 (print) | LCC HQ759.92 (ebook) | DDC 306.87--dc23

ISBN paperback: 978-0-578-33600-8
ISBN ebook: 978-0-578-33602-2

Printed in the United States of America

1 2 3 4 5 6 7 8 9 25 24 23 22

DEDICATION

I dedicate this book to all blended families.
My wish is that this book guides you to a meaningful
and lasting relationship.

*Look for small successes
and watch them grow.*

FOREWORD

By Elisabeth Davies

As a mental health counselor and author, I have had the opportunity to counsel many blended families over the past thirty-two years. I have witnessed many of the different struggles blended families have when building relationships between stepsiblings and a stepparent, specifically in communication and expectations. Newlywed single parents often do not communicate their different parenting expectations with their partner, regarding disciplining their children and stepchildren. They often don't discuss with their children how having a stepparent will impact them, while they are still grieving the loss of their original family. I have witnessed biological parents telling their children they do not have to listen to their new stepparent, resulting in sabotaging a blending family. Against my counsel, I have observed single parents getting ready to remarry not ask their children how they feel about their new stepparent, or how getting married will impact them. Sadly, these scenarios and many more are common to complicating, and even sometimes dissolving the blending of a family.

This does not stop that blended families are becoming more common each day. Thus Barbara Peters' book *Blended Families: Recipes for Success* comes at critical point in helping blended families thrive. The statistics show that second marriages are more likely to fail than first marriages. Reading and practicing the blended family skills in this book may lower that statistic!

Barbara Peters shares effective strategies that empower blended families to be successful, such as accepting change, building trust, listening with understanding, working together to create the family you desire, and good advice on what not to say about "exes". Barbara's recipe format is delightfully creative to read and practical to implement.

Barbara asks the reader to answer very important questions that can help decrease disaster in a blended family, such as What is a family for? How do we honor our biological parents, while making room in our hearts for a new parent? What are parents supposed to provide for their children? and What should happen if parents make mistakes? Answering these questions together as a blended family can guide parents and children to communicate together in healthy ways and create the family they desire.

I had the privilege of reading Barbara Peters' first book, *He Said, She Said, I Said: 7 Keys to Relationship Success*, in which she covered the skills to building a healthy relationship with a partner. Her relationship expertise shines through again in the strategies she shares in *Blended Families: Recipes for Success*. She wisely instructs the reader how to implement acceptance, trust, compassion, respect, flexibility, finances, communication, shared family identity, and couple intimacy, thus competently preparing any blended family to work well together.

Blended Families: Recipes for Success is most certainly a creatively illustrated and effectively written recipe for a successful blending of a family!

Elisabeth Davies, MC, mental health counselor and author of *Good Things Emotional Healing Journal: Addiction* and soon to be released *Good Things Emotional Healing Journal for Couples.*

PREFACE

This book is for you. This is a recipe book for success for blended families.

I wrote it to help prepare couples in second or third marriages who also have children, for the task of merging a family peacefully and successfully. I am a marriage counselor. I know the ingredients needed in a family. As a mother, a counselor, and coach, I have heard many stories about relationships. Most recently I have been focused on the blended family because I have seen and been a part of family divorces. The blended family is becoming, if not already, the family of the future. Most of my experience and expertise is in the field of relationships. I now recognize the extreme importance of helping the blended family to manage and overcome the obstacles that could prevent them from having a happily ever after.

My inspiration comes from the many couples I have counseled and my own family. My hope is to be a part of creating a new way to look at this type of relationship with a more positive outlook. I chose this topic because the high incidence of divorce today has created more second and third marriages than ever before, and there are few resources to help families through the many obstacles to creating a stable life. When I needed those resources myself, they just weren't there.

My life experience and personal history have been quite hard at times. I am currently working through blended family issues close to my heart. This work is not easy, but I am motivated to inspire others to forge through this often difficult transition to achieve personal well-being and a healthy family unit.

The purpose of this book is to show the critical components needed for a successful blended family that can co-exist in a healthy, loving manner. The recipe format is easy to follow. All of the material is intended to show you, the reader, a way to success.

CONTENTS

An Appetizer of What's to Come

Blended Families: Recipes for Success

I have written three books on relationships, and it's time to add another one on a topic that could not be more relevant. That is the topic of blended families, where a mom and dad are new to each other—but not new to marriage and the death or divorce of previous spouses. Blended families attempt to pull children from other marital situations into a new system, and it is not the easiest thing in the world to do well. In previous books, I mentioned blended families but sadly failed to give a recipe for a successful blend. I now want to do just that and give you the ingredients to make a successful transition into a happier two-parent home. In this book you will get new tools, and a new way to look at parenting.

Why is this topic of blended families so important these days?

According to an article by journalist Gail Rosenblum in 2018, half of weddings today create a stepfamily. She points out that about 41 percent of first marriages end in divorce. As for second marriages in which both partners have kids, the divorce rate is 70 percent. She goes on to say that common cited reasons that these marriages end include exes who interfere and children brought to the marriage.

Some people call these families by the terms stepfamily, blended family, bonus family, or instafamily. In this union, one parent (or both) has children who are not related to the other spouse, either biologically or by adoption. These children are from previous relationships or marriages.

Although the Covid-19 pandemic has caused a downward trend of both marriages and divorces, in general, blended families are becoming the predominant family structure in the United States and include both straight and gay parents. The blended family structure comes with a unique set of challenges that traditional marriage counseling and training may not address. Second, third, and more marriages are a fact of life in this country. For this reason alone, blended families are increasing in number.

The children from each past marriage go on to have a major impact on a new marriage. Whether they are adult children or much younger, they all cause challenges and add a new flavor to a marriage. If they will not accept Mom or Dad's new spouse, it dramatically increases the odds that a new marriage may not survive. But the fact is that many marriages have children from more than one father and mother. The resulting family system is indeed complicated and needs a special kind of union for it be a satisfying and lasting marriage.

Blended families: Harmony or hell?

This recipe book will provide ways to navigate the challenges in blending a family. It is a hands-on, easy guide for what to do and what not to do if you are in a blended family or thinking of being in one.

Being a product of a blended family, I have lots to say.

The relationship of the future has many blended family components, and this truth is mostly due to the high incidence of divorce and multiple marriages. The statistics tell all—but I am not going to bore you with more numbers and percentages, because that is not helpful. Besides, you can look those up on your own. What you can't look up is what you will read here: the recipe for getting through some of the biggest issues of blended families.

You are in a blended family. What did you not do, before you said "I Do"?

Did you talk about how you would deal with each other's children?

Did you talk about how you would deal with the "exes"?

Did you talk about your own child-rearing styles and ways of discipline?

Did you paint a picture of what it was like in your previous relationship with the children?

Did you clearly state your ideas of how to interact with the former parent and indicate how much of a presence that person would have in the new blended family?

Get my drift yet? If these things did not get discussed prior to marriage, there's no time like the present to get these ideas out in the open. Possibly you're just starting out in the union. Or possibly, you've hit the first snag. The more you know about each other's views, the more you may be able to see a solution that is the best fit for your unique situation.

Main Course:
Ingredients for a
Blended Family

ACCEPTANCE

SERVES: You, who are now in a blended family.

PREP: So maybe, before getting into this, you didn't ask all the questions that you could have or should have. Have no fear, just read on.

INGREDIENTS: Gently fold in redeeming qualities, boundaries, opportunities, and patience

READY: Acceptance is ready when you are. You do not need to become a doormat or a circus plate-spinner for everyone. You are still going to need to have some rules and some boundaries.

DIRECTIONS: Create a safe space in which change can occur. Sooner or later, if only out of curiosity, one of your new children will step into that space and take a closer look at you. If you want to be loved, first strive to deserve that love.

LET STAND: There are certain things that you cannot change. The sooner you stop trying, the better off you will be. You cannot change his or her children. They are who they are. They have a history with their birth mom or dad—a history you can't alter. You were not there. Find something good about each one of them and hold it close to your heart and memory.

COMBINE: DNA Stir-Fry is on the menu. You married their father or mother because you loved him or her. The DNA of your spouse is shared with their children. So each of them has redeeming qualities, just like the wonderful things you found in your spouse. Find and focus on them. Your task is to accept the things you cannot change and simply realize they are a part of the whole.

ARRANGE: Accept that the ex is a real family member, even if difficult. "Exes" have a legitimate need or reason for being involved with your new children. Whether they try to have input into your marriage is another matter!

RECIPE NOTES:

- ❤ *Warning!* One five-second, sarcastic remark can reverberate for years. Do not make any negative comments about the ex-spouse, grandparents, or other friends and relations.

- ❤ *Extreme caution!* Deceased spouses need to be handled with care. Accept that there was another parent who was loved and cared for, and that this love doesn't take anything away from your share of family affection.

TRUST

SERVES: When bringing many people together, doubt thrown into the recipe creates chaos and hurt feelings. Trust serves everyone. When someone in the family ignores the responsibility to follow a policy both of you have set, it leads to feelings of devaluation. The whole soufflé sinks!

PREP: Surprisingly, many couples never discuss trust prior to marriage. Trust in a blended family requires an open and honest disclosure of feelings. This is not a time to sit alone with your own thoughts. If the two of you can deeply consider each other's point of view, you can at least understand one another better, be kinder to one another, and face other people's agendas with determination to defend your own blended family.

- What did you both learn from your own parents about how to manage conflict?
- How do you each think children should be raised?
- How do you see the first spouse and stepchildren and their role in your new life together?

INGREDIENTS: Knead in **honor, reliability,** and **honest expression**

COOK UP SOME TRUST: Vow to make this marital alliance different.

READY: You've got the hang of it when the two of you stick together. Talk about what you need. Both of you set policy and then enforce it. If the two of you are allies, the family secures itself against divisive elements such as pushy exes or out-of-bounds children.

DIRECTIONS: If your partner knows a proposed boundary is reasonable, but he or she fears it can't be implemented, ask how you can help. Don't ask your partner for something that is hard for him or her unless it truly is important to you. Say why it matters so much that you are asking your loved one to step outside the comfort zone.

RECIPE NOTES: How Alliances Keep Conflict from Boiling Over

1. The two of you discuss honestly what the conflict is about. See it from your partner's point of view.

2. List the changes needed.

3. Give an example of how selling out the alliance might cause a division of family unity.

4. Agree to making changes and draw up a plan.

5. Follow through.

Bradford Veley, www.CartoonStock.com

COMPASSION

SERVES: Compassion is a tool to working with your partner and children.

PREP: A blended family recipe would be only half-baked without compassion. You'll need more than a teaspoon of it. I know, you have your own priorities, values, and emotions. How could other people possibly see things differently than you do? To figure that out, you'll need to put the crockpot on slow. Compassion will help you to slow down when you are having a difficult conversation with someone.

INGREDIENTS: Sauté with empathy and consideration

COOK: Temporarily put aside your values, thoughts, or ideas to consider what others hold dear to their heart.

READY: You're ready when you can look at your family members and imagine how they might feel.

DIRECTIONS: Perhaps your spouse is fearful of saying "no" to the kids and the ex. Have compassionate understanding of how your spouse feels. Perhaps he or she grew up in a family where he or she was fearful of not pleasing family members. Find out how he or she feels.

COMBINE: Sometimes extending compassion is a silent exercise. You can say a lot with a simple pat on the shoulder or a warm look of understanding. If your mate is dealing with an ex who is unreasonable, or children who are aggressive, you don't want to engage in a contest to see whether you can be even more unkind and difficult.

LET STAND: You may have married into a family of a widow/er. You desperately want to make it better. Know that when they grieve, they may simply want you to be there as a witness, allowing them time to recover from this painful life event. Offer your ability to listen.

TOSS GENTLY: Maybe your partner lacks boundaries. So often, in your opinion, the line is crossed. Put yourself in his or her place to see that it is not easy to change. Let him or her know why it is important to have boundaries. Make a plan together and then say, "I will support you on this plan."

RESPECT

SERVES: All members of the family can act in a way that shows they are aware of someone else's rights and wishes.

PREP: Cooking up a successful blended family cannot be done with a microwave approach. This is especially so with the ingredient of respect, which needs time to marinate. Respect is feeling admiration for someone. It means to regard someone as being worthy because of good qualities. Building respect takes awhile because it is earned by what you do.

INGREDIENTS: Knead in honor, reliability, and honest expression

ADD: Family members want to be respected for who they are and what they have accomplished. Most of all, we love to hear things such as "Job well done" or "I knew you could handle it."

READY: A blended family certainly makes life more challenging, with its complicated family structure. You will know you've got this when your family can stick to the simple things, respect each other, and when the bigger things do not seem as insurmountable.

DIRECTIONS: Don't let issues with a first marriage overshadow the happiness you want to experience now. You do have the courage and strength to face obstacles without falling into disrespect or disappointment. Patience instills self-confidence. Showing respect for others gains respect from others.

LET STAND: It is okay to speak your own thoughts without expecting that your partner will adopt your way of coping. You picked this individual because you admired his or her good qualities, and it is important to let your spouse know that you respect his or her choices.

SPOON OUT: When you set an example of respectfulness with young children, it will become their blueprint for how to handle their own lives. Even older children are constantly observing adults and gathering information about what their options are for facing conflict, setting their own goals, dealing with disappointment, or processing grief.

❤ *Caution!* Remind yourself that your spouse is a person with feelings and emotions. Your loved one was not put on Earth to simply do your bidding.

❤ *A husband or a wife* is not a hired hand; romance can only be kept alive when you feel good about yourself and good about them. Respect is the basis for mutual acceptance and kindness.

"I'M GLAD MOM MARRIED YOU, DAD, YOU'RE A STEPFATHER IN THE RIGHT DIRECTION."

Carroll Zan, www.CartoonStock.com

FLEXIBILITY

SERVES: Change brought the two of you together, and flexibility can help keep you together.

INGREDIENTS: Simmer well with willingness, adjustment, and compromise

PREP: When change comes, move with it, rather than against it.

COOK: Talk it through. Look at the pros and cons of keeping the status quo or making the change. It's a good idea for each of you to make a list of these factors and then trade them, so you can see the situation through someone else's eyes.

READY: Flexibility may not be comfortable. It places a priority on the "we" factor in the marriage. When can you achieve a "we" marriage? You are ready when you can think about your lives evolving into something new. Change requires an experimental attitude toward life.

DIRECTIONS: Get ready to dish out change. It would be tough to live well as a blended family without the willingness to adjust. As Dr. M. Scott Peck said in the twenty-fifth edition of his book *The Road Less Traveled,*

> *Once we truly know that life is difficult*
> *—once we truly understand and accept it—*
> *then life is no longer difficult. Because once it is accepted,*
> *the fact that life is difficult no longer matters.* (p. 15)

COMBINE: Just the two of you. Marital decisions should be made only by you and your spouse. Do not involve children—not even adult children. Some things are not their business!

LET STAND: Have a back-up plan if the change doesn't work. It isn't always possible to have a safety net; but if you can strategize together, partnership creates a cooperative family atmosphere.

ARRANGE: Put your options about your family on the table in order. Make small changes to practice for the bigger ones. This strategy keeps you in the habit of looking at life with fresh eyes. Tell your spouse if you are afraid to change. If your mate is slow to change, know what is especially difficult for your loved one, so that you can be more understanding.

SPOON OUT: A dollop of flexibility makes any family recipe smoother. You must be prepared to do something, to take action. If you both are not prepared to do something different, things will never change.

TOSS: Pitch any bitterness. Resentment by either one of you can snowball into distance, mistrust, and a growing reluctance to wholeheartedly invest in the marriage.

BLEND: Flexibility shows children a cohesive family structure. Remember, you are not only creating a marriage—you are also modeling adult relationships for your children. What impact do you want to have on them? Your marriage is a blueprint for their future.

FINANCE

SERVES: Finances can be tense for any parent. But deciding how to spend the family income on the blended kids can be like learning how to juggle flaming torches. Ideally, nobody will get burned once we have shed some light on this topic.

ADD AS ZEST: planning, assigning tasks, seeking professional advice

COMBINE: You want to have a joint account. What's involved?

- If you have a joint account, all decisions about where that money goes ought to be made together. The decision to pool resources is a huge one. If you have a partner who does not record spending or won't stay within limits, you won't have the trust that is necessary to keep your household afloat. Agree to clear communication, clear goals and procedures, and mutual responsibility.

- If you are sharing your money as a couple, decide exactly what that means. Does it mean anything goes with that account, or are there checks and balances on it? For instance, is there a limit on how much you spend on Christmas gifts for both families of children, now living as one family? Do the gifts come from shared money or from separate accounts? Who pays for school tuition and other educational expenses? Do the children get an allowance, and if so, from which parent? Because unforeseen demands can arise, it may be a good idea to have a regularly scheduled meeting between the two of you so that you know you have a time set aside to resolve such matters. If you happen to be crisis-free on any given week, the meeting can always turn into a session of mutual compliments and favorite beverages.

TO BLEND OR NOT TO BLEND: Couples who put their resources into one blended family crockpot to simmer tend to be happier. For instance, many couples open a joint account where they deposit money for household expenses such as the mortgage, utilities, and groceries. But maybe you are used to managing your own money. Perhaps you don't like how your spouse tracks expenses, and you feel out of control when you think of putting everything into one crockpot. It's enough to make you unravel a dishtowel! If so, consider keeping your own checking account and bookkeeping system, but always tell the truth about finances to your spouse.

ARRANGE: You've got child support. A major expense! Is that a separate expense, or are each of you contributing to the other's obligations? Usually child support is paid to the custodial parent and comes out of separate finances. This is also true of alimony payments and legal fees. Ex-spouses often have conflict over these matters, and sometimes these differing opinions wind up in family court. Remember to keep children out of these conflicts. They're too young to understand that of course adults might differ in opinion. The divorce agreement may need to be flexible for the kids. If you are in a bind with issues around support, you could try a therapist or go to mediation. Have courage and don't put off saving for college; financial advisers can help.

PLACE: Put anxiety to rest. A family law attorney can help you if you feel that your divorce left you hanging by a financial thread:

- If you've lost money in the divorce.
- Or the divorce left you without adequate child support.
- Or you believe your alimony payments are too much.

SPOON OUT: Who is going to balance the checkbooks, and how often? Who will pay each bill? How will you compile your expenses for tax payment purposes? Don't be afraid to go over each item on the agenda of family finances and clarify who does what and when. It's also important to prevent problems by making yourself available to help out or function as a backup if your significant other is ill, overwhelmed, or unusually busy at work. Don't protect a growing problem by refusing to ask for help! Sharing information about how everything functions can be crucial in case of emergencies like a sudden layoff or critical health problems.

DEFROST: Take your future out of the freezer. Make an investment in your upcoming life.

- Together, figure out what your income is and the biggest of the expenses.
- Then write down what you dream about for the future. He wants to add on to the garage to accommodate a classic car. You think of vacationing in an exotic place. And in your retirement, you want the two of you to travel. An advisor can help you save to retire.

It's not only what we say that matters.
It's how we say it that makes the difference.

COMMUNICATION

SERVES: Everyone. In your new blended family, your communication skills may need a makeover. The new family is not where you lived before and may seem like no easy picnic. Although communicating in a blended family is something that can get better with time, keep your recipe simple enough to follow easily without bailing out. It is not only the content of the message that counts. You cannot simply text the kids that dinner is ready. It is the delivery that makes the difference, so be mindful of your tone and choice of words.

"... I'd been used to driving our family car on country roads,
puttering along nice and easy,

taking the curves with caution and experienced control.
Now, all of a sudden,

I find myself driving a semi-truck during the
Los Angeles rush hour.

I may have done quite well before, but I'm not on
country roads anymore.

I have taken the ramp to a superhighway..."

— Tom and Adrienne Frydenger,
from *Resolving Conflict in the Blended Family*

PREP: Too many cooks can upend the stew! You may have stepkids who don't accept you as an authority figure or a nurturer, and perhaps a meddling ex-spouse to contend with in addition to a whole new set of beliefs about parenting. You need to tell your partner how you feel. You can say this without seeming attacking and critical. I do not mean forget it and keep your mouth shut. Certainly, do not gloss over what you see as destructive or outrageous. If you don't express how you are feeling, it will become part of your burden of resentment later on. So by all means, speak up! Having private time to talk to your new spouse is imperative. "Let's check in with each other" is one way to make communication regular.

COOK: Keep the goal in view. Let your new spouse know how important it is to create a loving family with his or her kids. Say how you want to include the kids in the new family. Study their interests and priorities.

READY: To get ready, consider how your partner reacts to hearing negatives about his or her children. Also, tread lightly on the topic of ex-spouses. Maybe their biological mom is a gourmet cook. Your goal is not to replace her. By making a reference to one of her positive qualities, you establish yourself as a perceptive person who is not trying to compete. You can create a breathing space for your own presence in these people's lives.

WHISK TO INCORPORATE: delivery of the message, timing, listening

DIRECTIONS: One useful way to communicate an idea for change is, "When x happens, I feel y. So I want you to do z, and this is what I am going to try." What if you need your spouse to be more direct with his or her kids and set better limits? If they have never done that before, you might need to give them some reasons why it would help. At all costs, however, refrain from being a know-it-all.

LET STAND: Be willing to see the other's perspective even if you don't agree. There is always something to learn. The ideal would be to incorporate the best of both methods to avoid undue disagreement.

SET THE TIMER FOR SUCCESS: Choose your timing to have a serious discussion. Exploding or falling apart when the family is on their way to an important event is not going to give you much chance of being heard. You may have to hold your tongue until the kids are asleep or out doing their own thing.

ADD: Be a good listener. Ask questions if you do not understand some of your spouse's behavior and his or her difficulty when changes need to be made. Ask how you might do better. A team is only as good as all the players working together.

TOSS: Be reasonable with your needs. Learn to let go of the things that you can accept even if they are not your first choice.

A blended family is value-added. Enjoy its benefits.

SHARED FAMILY IDENTITY

SERVES: Family members are those who have "bought into" a group of people related by blood, love, social custom, family custom, purpose, and law. A shared identity creates the credibility and security of the new family. The children should see this sharing early on in your newly formed marriage.

PREP: Like holiday bread, blended family lives are braided together in a fresh pattern. Family tradition guides us as we struggle to live ethical and decent lives.

TIME TO COMPLETE: If it takes several months or even a few years for the family process to run smoothly, that's not unusual. Parenting additional children is a major adjustment. I know you may feel like you have been transported onto an out-of-control train. When you two discuss your new roles of parenting, each of you is entitled to volunteer for certain tasks within the family and decline others.

CARAMELIZE UNTIL GOLDEN: customs, tradition, security

DIRECTIONS: It may be best if the biological parent takes the lead in dealing with disobedience by his or her children. But as soon as there is a parental bond made by the children with the new parent, then the new parent should be empowered to guide the younger members of the family.

COMBINE: Successful parents back each other up and present a united front. It really helps if you and your spouse work as allies, taking private time for you two to discuss things. Your children's biological parent may have left behind a legacy of beliefs, policies, and emotions that weigh heavily on your new family. You would like to do things according to your sense of how parents should relate to one another and to their offspring. It may seem as if any decision you make is compared to your predecessor's habits and found wanting. It can take a ton of patience to get through the inevitable period of adjustment. Conflict in front of "the kids" should be kept to a minimum.

♥ *Caution!* Trying to buy children's affection with gifts, indulgence, or flattery may only teach them how to use adults against one another. Trying to play the same role that your predecessor played will not allow you and your spouse to create a unique relationship that reflects the flavor of your love.

LET STAND: It means so much to your spouse and the children to know that you love them unconditionally. Children may deny that they reciprocate your concern. But this rebellion is normal, especially for teenagers who may be trying to differentiate from their family of origin while not being quite ready for adult autonomy. The older your children are, the more they can be included in the process of creating a new family identity, with new traditions, a team that has room for all the adult authority figures. A blended family is an opportunity for children to learn new ways of bonding, loving, nurturing, and conflict resolution.

"Happy Father's Day....send all."

Martha Campbell, www.CartoonStock.com

TOSS: Get rid of the pressure cooker. Going to sleep with resentment in your heart won't do anything to solve your problems. Speak up, trust that there will be a solution, and see what happens next. There may not be a quick improvement; but as long as you are loved and able to give love, your place in your new family will be valid and can grow. The advice in this recipe book is not to live inside a pressure cooker. Instead, be patient with each other, because developing a family identity is not a race.

REFRIGERATE: The fridge is a great spot for a family mission statement. Kids can help so that everyone is in this together. They will learn that it is okay to say how they feel. Children who were disappointed by a divorce may want to distance themselves from that pain. A new parent can be blamed for disrupting the family. This possibility makes it crucial to have good boundaries and rules that are clearly stated.

- What is a family for?

- What are parents supposed to provide for their children?

- What are the rights and responsibilities of the children?

- How do we honor our biological parents, while making room in our hearts for a new parent?

- What should happen when children make mistakes?

- What should happen if parents make mistakes?

- What are our goals as a family?

- What are our values?

- How do we express those values in our daily lives?

When the Going Gets Tough,
Blended Families Gather Courage

When you are in doubt, ask yourself,

"What is the most loving thing I can do in this situation?"

If you need to bring a concern to your spouse or offer
some criticism, preface it with,

"I want you to know how much I love you."

COUPLE INTIMACY

BUILD A BATTER AND THEN POUR IN: love, rapport, pleasure, connection

SERVES: This one is for the two of you. Being intimate is allowing someone to know you for who you are, without judging you. When there is intimacy, there is trust; and where there is trust, there may be all kinds of mutual and pleasurable experiences. Sexual expression is usually part of a couple's way of literally making or creating love. But it's important to pay attention to other forms of intimacy as well. Consideration for your partner can lead to a willingness to revel in physical connections.

PREP: You married this person. But over time, your issues, your ex-spouse's issues, and the kids' issues could make the togetherness between you two look like something barely visible in your car's rear view mirror. Couples with blended families who stay together are able to keep a sense of humor about a partner's foibles or shortcomings. There is an atmosphere of flexibility and respect for each other's unique points of view.

CREATE: In intimacy, the efforts of two people are required. If your partner is kind, accepting, and aroused by your erotic requests, don't leave him or her hanging in a state of indifference or being put down. You aren't required to do everything your partner may want you to do. But you are invited to understand and affirm your partner's value.

READY: Be ready to trust. In order to be intimate, we must be exposed. We can only get close to someone who is also taking a risk and being vulnerable. Most of us don't feel that love is complete unless we know that the other person needs us. Allow yourself to give and receive pleasure. This is the surest way to keep each other close and cement your bond with one another. Every couple has their own ways to reciprocate physically. On some days, a massage fits the bill better than a sexual finale. Feeling taken care of, and being able to give your partner care, are essential.

DIRECTIONS: Spend awhile together alone without kids, phones, dogs, or work. Choose a place to be alone with each other every single day. Most of the time, that might look like a quick kiss in the kitchen before dinner is served or a little pillow-talk once the kids are asleep. But don't forget to create special occasions—a long walk, a dinner for two, a visit to a favorite bookstore, or going somewhere. Make it an event to talk about the two of you.

LET STAND: Children may complain if left with a sitter. Yet go on dates without guilt.

CREATE A NEW MENU: You are a new couple and are creating your own closeness. Find out what pleases your partner sexually. Ask. Don't assume that you know. Be honest about your needs. Between two consenting adults, there are a multitude of options for teasing and pleasing each other. Give honest feedback about how any given touch or technique feels, and try new things. Make sure you don't discuss your histories with other partners, and never compare your spouse to your ex. (It helps if neither of you asks pointed questions about each other's sexual experiences in the past.)

💙 *Caution!* Are you starting to feel like daily life has become all about the kids, work, finances, or an ex-spouse? Then get childcare and make time to feel close to one another. When you function as a team, then facing chores or changes is much easier.

ADD MORE THAN A DASH OF TRUTH: If you feel you have an awful secret, or you are afraid your partner will be upset if he or she hears a difficult truth, just think about this. Your marriage can adapt to conflict or unfinished business. That's actually pretty normal. But a marriage can't survive dishonesty or a sense that the other person is absent.

AVOID CARRY OUT: Looking for sympathy elsewhere? Don't discuss marital conflicts with your children or an ex-partner. It can be very tempting to seek out sympathy from people outside of your marriage. We all need support, but there are ways to get it that don't betray the confidence of your new husband or wife. Problems become much harder to solve if private difficulties become a topic for gossip, or if third parties try to "help" or use a small problem to drive a wedge between the two of you.

TOSS: Leaving old patterns behind is your best strategy for continuing to be intimate. You probably have a sense of what did not work in your previous marriage. Take care of resentments. Don't allow a grievance to sour. Create space in your relationship to air disappointments, doubts, or anger.

Writing Exercise for Couples in a Blended Family

Separately, each person writes down a brief answer to these questions. If you like, you can share these messages with each other. But you do not have to share. Instead, together you can burn the papers and resolve to make a new beginning.

1. What did I learn about marriage from my previous one?

2. What did I find out about my sexuality from my previous marriage?

———

Possible answers would be, "I learned to feel shy about my body," or "I came to believe I wanted more than I was ever going to get."

The Sweet Course

When the past sours your recipe

The course of a blended family through time can be as sweet as a sugar cookie but may at other points resemble rocky road ice cream. Blending takes awhile, and in fact blended families may always be evolving. This last section will look at married life, with my best hopes for the rough patches.

There is a common stumbling block that couples in blended families share: bringing their past into the current relationship. This mistake can be infuriating, but it makes sense that we base our fears about the future on past experience.

But the truth is, we don't have to be trapped within the cycles of the past. A new relationship is an opportunity to create greater freedom and trust. Nothing in the world says that a new love will fall into old patterns. The problem is that when people believe problematic conduct will be repeated, they are looking for it. Suspicion and pessimism can take the exhilaration out of your romance. When such issues become perpetual, they must be put to rest.

For the sake of practicality, I offer
the following suggestions:

1. Watch your spouse's behavior and look for the positive. Compliment him or her on their good actions and intentions. Suspend any thoughts of comparing him or her to another. Look only at what you see and what is real in the here and now.

2. Keep away from any conversations about what has happened in the past. Focus on the conversation you are having today, not yesterday. Think about how you can make each day the best possible day for you, your spouse, and the kids.

3. If your spouse brings up a conversation about his or her

former relationships, don't engage. Use friendly reminders that you are not the same person as the former spouse. Bring the conversation to the issue at hand.

4. Remain calm and focus on each other.

5. Have a vision for your family's future and talk as a group about your hopes and goals, not the failures or shortcomings of the past. Plan new adventures and life experiences that you will share. List the benefits of your new life together as a blended family.

6. Show your love and respect for each other. Romantic verbal expressions are great, but you need to back them up with considerate actions.

Sometimes the cake won't rise, no matter what you do

What if a dish doesn't turn out well, despite all the steps being followed to a "T"? You may feel frustrated that your effort didn't produce the desired result. Fortunately, you can try it again. But when the recipe is for marriage, and there may be children depending on you for stable parenting, making changes is not as simple as cooking a new dish. So what is next?

Here is my suggestion: Be friends. Yes! Decide to be friends and do whatever you both decide to do, with the kids in mind. You can resolve the problem by fixing it or changing the relationship. You don't have to have the same marriage as your parents, years ago. You don't have to follow the rules that everybody else seems to find so easy to obey. What "a good relationship" or "happiness" means is up to both of you.

Maybe it means you simply have a friendly marriage. Maybe it means you get a "friendly" divorce. Perhaps you both just step back a bit and start again as friends first. You can redefine what it means to be friends. No matter what you choose, more can be gained in a pleasant manner instead of an adversarial one. Little is gained with anger or hostility.

We may not know exactly what we should do, but we are going to find out, and we will do this together. We care about each other a lot, and we are on the same side.

Keep blame out of the brew. No one is perfect or all-knowing. If there are problems, your spouse may be in the same pickle that you are in—looking for a way out, self-blaming, not being sure if there is an escape.

My hope is that this recipe book for blended families will help you to create a happy, long-lasting family and that you will have resounding success. I would love to feel that many of you who are reading this book will never need to think about how to stay together during troubled times.

But (as I well know), things can go wrong. I would be remiss in letting you all believe that the words on these pages are magic. So I won't do that. I do know, however, that these words and pages can make a difference in blending your family for the better. I know this because I am doing it, too. Yes, it is hard work. But it's work that is well worth it.

When teens turn prickly

Perhaps your teen shows anger or withdrawal, particularly about the divorce and remarriage. They may have divided loyalties and resent interference from a new person. Listen to their feelings about their new life. Offer your patience for this confusing, worrisome time. Remember that all teens are struggling with becoming their own person, so some angst at this age is normal. As you work to become closer, keep in mind that you will also soon be

letting go. Explain to them that they can always come to you, no matter what the trouble is. If they are feeling peer pressure about drugs or sex, tell them to use you as the excuse. Tell them they can say, "My parents won't let me do that."

Children want to know you have their back. The best thing for their future is to see the important adults in their life cheering them on. When parents show interest and offer praise, children gain confidence. If teens see teamwork among adults, they can learn by example. If they observe how you manage to face difficult things, they will understand how to handle problems. This could be the basis of their success and happiness in life.

If you wanted things to be perfect but they weren't

If you are looking for a marriage to be perfect, look again. In an ideal world, we would all be happy, and self-help books probably wouldn't be necessary. The truth is, we don't have a perfect marriage all the time. If you are thinking of abandoning your relationship because it is not perfect, here are some things to consider.

Lifelong commitment takes looking away from the small annoyances. For example:

Your spouse doesn't put things away. You are constantly picking up his socks.

You get annoyed because his ex always calls at a bad time.

His kids often come in and don't wipe their feet.

Without consulting you, he used a gift card from your parents on a new rod and reel to go fishing with your teen.

He likes to cuddle, but you sleep close to the edge.

Because he makes math errors, you have to balance the checkbook.

I am sure there are other minor annoyances because after all, you are two different people and have come from two different worlds. Keep in mind the reasons why you picked him as your special partner. I often talk about a "relationship agreement" and it goes something like this:

I agree to keep my relationship as my utmost priority and work on it every day. I will not allow any cause to be a reason to forget my agreement. It is my hope that my everlasting love for you, along with this agreement, will help us achieve a relationship that will be the loving center of our blended family.

Remind yourself of his cute smile, how he helps when you are tired.

Think of how she cooked your favorite meal.

Remind yourself of how she listened to you after a hard day at the office.

The two of you must able to navigate the rough spots and come out on top with a positive outcome. It may not happen instantly; but with perseverance, you will surely get there and be thankful that you didn't throw it away over small stuff.

"As our love for each other flows on in all its changing forms—easy and tense—we grow up. And that's the goal with all of this, isn't it? Growing up and learning to see and accept our families for what they are, rather than getting stuck in our individual and preconceived ideas about what 'family' should be like. Your family 'should' be just as it is— ever changing and delicious."

— Ariel Gore, in Samantha Waltz's
Blended: Writers on the Step-family Experience

Write me!

I would like so much to hear from you. Write to me about your blended family. I can be contacted through barbarajpeters.com. Thanks for reading and giving these ideas a chance! Blessings on us all for trying to be good, loving people who wake up each day resolved to do our best and live according to our deepest values. May we all know joy and have memories of happiness.

REFERENCES

Covey, Stephen. 1997. *The 7 Habits of Highly Effective Families.* New York: St. Martin's Press, Golden Books.

Frydenger, Tom and Adrienne. 1991. *Resolving Conflict in the Blended Family.* Ada, MI: Chosen Books.

Gore, Ariel. 2015. Foreword. In Samantha Waltz's 2015 *Blended: Writers on the Stepfamily Experience.* Berkeley, CA: Seal Press.

Peck, M. Scott. 1978. *The Road Less Traveled,* p. 15 in the 25th ed., 2003. New York: Simon & Schuster.

Pew Research Center. Oct. 1–21, 2010. *Social and Demographic Trends Survey.* Washington, DC: Pew.

Rosenblum, Gail. Jan. 28, 2018. The link between stepkids and divorce—And how you can beat the odds. *Star Tribune,* Variety section.

Smart Stepfamilies. 2016. Little Rock, AR: FamilyLife Blended, https://smartstepfamilies.com/

Britan, a Cavalier King Charles Spaniel, shown with the author, Barbara J. Peters. Together they bring cheer to those in assisted living.

ABOUT THE AUTHOR

Barbara J. Peters is a successful author and relationship coach. For many years she specialized in relationship counseling as a licensed professional counselor. In her first book, *The Gift of a Lifetime: Building a Marriage that Lasts*, she lends insight from her experience as a couples' counselor. Her second book, *He Said, She Said, I Said*, focuses directly on the issues of communication from the perspectives of the couple and the counselor.

Barbara received a Bachelor of Arts in sociology from C.W. Post College of Long Island University, a Bachelor of Science in nursing from Stony Brook University, and she earned a Master of Science in counseling from Georgia State University. She is a registered nurse, is certified by the National Board of Certified Counselors and is a former member of the Licensed Professional Counselors of Georgia.

A Long Island native, Barbara resides in the Charlotte area of North Carolina with her husband, but frequently visits Alpharetta, Georgia, where she lived for many years. She is devoted to her family, which includes two grown daughters, four grandchildren, and a therapy dog, a Cavalier King Charles Spaniel, that brings smiles to those in assisted living.

She is passionate about helping people improve their relationships. Through her books and blog (barbarajpeters.com), she focuses on assisting couples to make positive changes. Her hope is that readers will gain useful skills that are easy to incorporate into their daily living.

ACKNOWLEDGMENT

I have one person to thank. Jan Hall has been my editor and friend for many years. Her excellent editing and impeccable attention to detail has been greatly appreciated. Throughout these years she has been understanding and accepting of my unique personality. She was patient when I asked many questions and changed my mind frequently. She brings a wealth of knowledge, which is unsurpassed. No question is left unanswered. She is there when I need her and always has a smile on her face. Her enthusiasm and encouragement kept me on track to bring my vision to my words. Thank you, Jan, you made the difference.

OTHER BOOKS BY BARBARA J. PETERS

The Gift of a Lifetime, Building a Marriage That Lasts

This book is based on the FACTS and how they contribute to having a lifetime marriage:

F is for Forgiveness

A is for Acceptance

C is for Compassion

T is for Trust

S is for Spirituality

It provides case studies of "real couples" seen in counseling. Included is a page for the bride and groom to write a love letter to each other and compose a wedding vow. This book would be a thoughtful gift for any couple getting ready to tie the knot.

ISBN 978-1-4490-4658-3

He Said She Said I Said, 7 Keys to Relationship Success

Learn about the various perspectives and misconceptions that couples encounter. Find answers and new ways to navigate the differences, which can be turned into shared meanings. With this guide, you will know how to reframe the way you see interactions and situations in your own relationships.

ISBN 978-0-983-16998-7

Never Too Old for Romance

Finally, a romance novel about a mature woman. The heroine takes risks, grows, and makes a crucial decision: to end up alone if it means being true to herself. Read about her journey, a story that you will not forget and that will surprise you along the way.

ISBN 978-0-615-81076-8

ONE MORE RECIPE: YOURS!

Some people follow a recipe exactly as it is written. Others decide to tweak it. Which one do you prefer?

Recipes are, at best, a guide. Usually if one is followed exactly, the dish comes out well. Occasionally, even if followed exactly, a recipe may not be quite to your taste. Maybe it needs a little jolt of hot sauce.

Here is your chance to tweak the recipes in this book to your individual needs. In the next few pages are ideas and suggestions to create your Blended Family recipe. I hope you will use the information in this book as examples for your own. Of course, if you are satisfied with the ones provided, then go for it. But you can make changes to fit your unique situation.

These pages are intended for you to write in this book, or in some cases post on your refrigerator or bulletin board, to remind you of the daily recipe for success. You may cut them out or copy them from the book. Put one of these in a place where you will see it each day as a reminder of the work involved in creating a successful blended family.

ACCEPTANCE

What is the most important thing you can do for acceptance to happen today?

Your thoughts:

_____

_____

_____

_____

Your partner's thoughts:

I need to accept

_____

_____

_____

You need to accept

_____

_____

_____

We need to accept

_____

_____

_____

TRUST

Most relationships struggle with this one. Is there anything that caught your eye in our recipe for this ingredient? Trust is a small word but a big request. Think about what you need to trust your spouse each day. Is it about finances? Is it about parenting styles? Is it about the role your ex needs to occupy in your blended family?

Now you pick.

Your request:

_____

_____

_____

Your spouse's request:

_____

_____

_____

Your mutual request:

_____

_____

_____

COMPASSION

We all need empathy and concern from our loved one at times, and on some occasions more than others. Giving compassion is about getting outside of your own needs and being able to see or understand the needs of another. Acknowledge each other's agendas.

Write one way you can show compassion today.

_____

_____

_____

Have your spouse do the same.

_____

_____

_____

Ask questions and pose one here. For example, how do you want to receive compassion today?

_____

_____

_____

How can each of you practice kindness today?

_____

_____

_____

How does your spouse want to receive compassion today?

_____

_____

_____

What is unique about your spouse?

_____

_____

_____

What do you see as your spouse's vulnerabilities and need for support at this phase in your relationship?

_____

_____

_____

Have your spouse answer this question as well.

_____

_____

_____

Are each of you on the mark, or do you want to offer additional information? Keep each other in the loop about what you need!

_____

_____

_____

RESPECT

Building respect in your blended family involves being supportive of another's point of view. How do you each do this?

_____

_____

How can you offer support or validation to your spouse today?

_____

_____

Have your spouse answer this question as well.

_____

_____

Do you need to offer more recognition or affirmation to your children? Both you and your spouse can answer this question.

_____

_____

What are challenges your children have faced in joining a blended family?

_____

_____

What have they done well?

_____

_____

FLEXIBILITY

Life is a process of perpetual change and growth. Being able to change course or compromise is an important ingredient in successfully blending a family to strengthen your relationship.

_____

_____

_____

What makes it difficult for you to compromise or change course?

_____

_____

What might make it easier for you to do this?

_____

_____

Ask your spouse to answer the same question here.

_____

_____

_____

FINANCE

Money matters can be the cause of much conflict. It is also a topic difficult to discuss openly and honestly.

Each of you can prepare your own budgets and then share them with your spouse. Incorporate the best of both and come up with a blended budget.

Be careful to consider merging family responsibilities for the children's needs. Write that information here.

_____

_____

_____

_____

_____

_____

What were the most difficult parts of creating or agreeing to a budget for you? For your spouse?

_____

_____

_____

_____

_____

_____

COMMUNICATION

Communication is the glue that can hold a marriage together. Distorted messages or a lack of contact can destroy the bliss you are trying to savor. But it is rare for two people to speak to each other same way, even if they have the best of intentions.

What is your communication style? For example, do you disclose sensitive information easily, or do you bottle things up to avoid conflict?

_____

_____

_____

How does your spouse answer this question?

_____

_____

_____

Each of you can name one thing that might make communication flow more openly.

_____

_____

_____

Now "blend" the two. Take the best parts of each individual statement and create a new and improved way to keep each other updated. Maybe using "I" statements works; maybe asking more questions works; maybe repeating and reframing a statement is helpful; or perhaps good eye contact and listening more is what is needed. Successful contact is the part that counts most for the recipe to come out "perfect."

Name one communication skill your partner is good at that you wish you could learn. Both of you could answer this.

_____

_____

Pick three things that are crucial to do each day as you communicate with one another.

1. _____

2. _____

3. _____

Individual personality types play into our expertise with various challenges. Does one of you have more patience than the other?

_____

Is one of you better at handling an unpleasant conflict with a third party?

_____

Does one of you tend to take over when a child is upset?

_____

Who feels competent around taxes and other financial issues?

_____

Both of you could answer, then you both could discuss which one of you might manage certain areas of the relationship and interfacing with the outside world.

SHARED FAMILY IDENTITY

You might have been making chicken parmesan once a week all your adult life until you blended your family. Now, you are cooking for a group of people who would rather have spaghetti.

Write about something that changed for you because you became part of a blended family.

_____

_____

_____

How does your spouse answer this question?

_____

_____

_____

What can you do to adapt to your blended family's specific preferences or needs?

_____

_____

_____

How does your spouse answer this question?

_____

_____

_____

Refer back to the recipe for some guidance if needed.

Build a family mission statement with your children. Talk to them about why you would like to make one. According to business professor Stephen Covey, "A family mission statement is a combined, unified expression from all family members of what your family is about—what it is you really want to do and be—and the principles you choose to govern your family life" (p. 70). It can show what is important to all of you. Family members with a shared identity think in terms of "us" rather than always just "me." Working together always has more potential because of our differences. For example, some values that might be in the mission statement include:

Adventure	Fun	Spirituality
Creativity	Health	Integrity
Discipline	Honesty	Kindness
Education	Humor	Service

COUPLE INTIMACY

This is our final ingredient. Now you get to create your intimate relationship. This is an adult space for your interactions as a couple. You don't have to do any writing exercises here. But high-quality intimacy does not happen without mutual effort and compatibility! How can you improve this part of your life? Find out what your mate wants and needs. Be open and vulnerable in discussing this topic. Share what works for you and what doesn't. Have meaningful conversations. This does not get posted on the refrigerator. It is only for the two of you. Enjoy each other. Give and receive love.

CPSIA information can be obtained
at www.ICGtesting.com
Printed in the USA
BVHW061302260122
627256BV00015B/268

9 780578 336008